Cold calls to hot leads

THE SALES LEADERSHIP SERIES – PART I

Nicholas McMenemy

Sandholme Publishing

SYDNEY, AUSTRALIA

Copyright © 2014 by Nicholas McMenemy.

All rights reserved. No part of this publication may be reproduced, distributed or transmitted in any form or by any means, including photocopying, recording, or other electronic or mechanical methods, without the prior written permission of the publisher, except in the case of brief quotations embodied in critical reviews and certain other non-commercial uses permitted by copyright law. For permission requests, write to the publisher, addressed "Attention: Permissions Coordinator," at the address below.

Nicholas McMenemy/Sandholme Publishing
396 George Street, Sydney, NSW, 2001
www.sandholme-publishing.com

Special discounts are available on quantity purchases by corporations, associations, and others. For details, contact the "Special Sales Department" at the address above.

Cold calls to hot leads/ Nicholas McMenemy — 2nd ed.
ISBN 978-1- 5030-8039-3

Contents

Becoming a sales leader begins with a first call 1

The journey starts with self-discovery 4

    What makes this book different? 6

    Do I need to read the entire book, cover to cover? 7

    How long before I begin to see an improvement? 8

Defining what success looks like 9

The first step on the path to excellence 14

    What if I don't have prior ratios to compare? 18

    How will I know when I am improving? 19

Farming the most fertile soil 24

    Determining other segments to target 27

Defining the universe 30

    Competitor customers 34

    Data, data everywhere, but where do I start? 35

The first step to success – starting! 38

    Cleaning the data 41

    What if the company has a no-names policy? 42

Why do they keep saying "No"? 43

Just one more piece of homework 44

Planning your pitch 48

The most effective time to call 49

Knowing what to say when you do get through 51

Tailoring the message for different audiences 56

Ask for that appointment 57

Practice, Practice, Practice 58

Success starts now 64

Making the call 65

Communication in action 66

Timing the call 67

"No" or "Send me more information" 68

They are never there and never call me back 70

Leaving voicemail 72

Gordon Gekko 78

A life less ordinary 80

Dedicated to Emily, Eliza and Hugo for your continued support, laughter and guidance

For Stuart who has encouraged, laughed and worked to tease this from me

And Kerri for keeping me on track

*Until one is committed
there is hesitancy, the chance to draw back
always ineffectiveness.
Concerning all acts of initiative and creation
there is one elementary truth
the ignorance which kills countless
ideas and splendid plans:
The moment that one definitely commits one's self
then Providence moves too.
All sorts of things occur to help one
that would never otherwise have occurred.
A whole stream of events issues from the decision
raising in one's favour all manner
of unforeseen incidents and meetings
and material substance
which no one could have dreamt
would have come their way.
Whatever you can do or dream you can, begin it.
Boldness has genius, power and magic in it.*

— GOETHE

PREFACE

Becoming a sales leader begins with a first call

We live in a time renowned for the pace of innovation and change. What was considered ground-breaking 6 months ago, is now considered standard procedure and common-place, against which we all run hard and harder. And what we accomplish today will soon be forgotten as we strive to compete ever-more vigorously with new competitors, for new customers, in new ways.

Businesses that survive and prosper will be those that are able to ultimately maintain and grow a strong sales pipeline both through selling more to existing customers and delighting them, but also through their ability to keep filling their sales pipeline with qualified opportunities and leads, that ultimately convert to sales and revenue.

The process of filling that sales pipeline with appointments is a function of one thing – hard work. As any sales manager will tell you

"SALES IS A NUMBERS GAME"

Slight modifications to the way in which each of us behaves and works each day can have a massive impact on our performance and professional success.

This book focuses on activities that will help you modify and ultimately improve your performance. It will provide you with a series of tools to maximise your appointment-setting effectiveness – data selection tools, value-proposition creation and targeting, scripts for calling and voicemail, and process management tools. Use and personalize these tools as directed and you will see a significant improvement in your sales performance.

Throughout this book I have certain terms that are used to identify prospects or customers throughout the sales cycle. The terminology is fairly simple to understand and should be fairly logical to anyone who is engaged in the whole process of sales, but just in case and for the sake of consistency, here are the definitions:

- Suspect – A company or individual who may have an interest in your product or service, but has yet to be qualified as being interested
- Prospect – A company or individual who has shown a positive interest in wanting to know more about your product or service and, who is in a position to make a purchasing decision when budgets are available

- Lead – A company or individual who is in a purchasing cycle and is considering your company as one of their potential suppliers. They have Budget, are Authorised to spend, have a defined and known Need, and a defined Timeframe in which they will need or want to make decisions (BANT qualified)

I recognize that different industries will have different terms that mean the same thing, but feel it important to establish a common language that provides a framework for learning, discussion and action.

Now that you understand the terminology, you are in a position to start making massive progress.

CHAPTER 1

The journey starts with self-discovery

Even if you don't think you are, everybody is selling something to somebody each day – be it ourselves, something manufactured for sale, or acted as an agent for somebody else, we are all selling and it is an integral part of our daily lives – we simply cannot avoid it.

This book helps you focus on doing the optimal amount of work to generate the best possible return for the funnel-building activity that you conduct, generate sales and meet targets. It is a simple guide to make sure that each and every sales call you make, generates either a qualified appointment or a sale. You can even use this approach when searching for a new role, it is that flexible.

We often hear the sales truism outlined earlier that "Sales is a numbers game". The simple belief that the more people who know

THE JOURNEY STARTS WITH SELF DISCOVERY

about your product or service, the more people will consider buying it and the more sales you make – simple right? Well not quite. It is only part of the entire sales equation and misses many key elements that are essential if you are to become a true sales achiever.

In the increasingly competitive world of business, the average sales person will likely secure a single sales appointment after having called between 30-250 contacts. Let's consider that and what it means:

- Each of those calls takes approximately 3 minutes (including set up times, actually dialling, post call warm down)
- That's between 90 - 750 minutes of solid calling to generate each appointment
- Meaning that to secure a meeting can take at least 1.5 hours of calling time to secure

On that basis, a whole 9-hour working day might generate 6 meetings - chances are you'll miss your target as there aren't enough hours in the day to secure all the meetings you need to be successful, in addition to following up on all the appointments you may have made is previous days.

But that is only part of the equation. Some sales people stop at this point, accept that they have to call a lot to get appointments and continue on regardless. This book provides tools so that you not only analyse the number of calls that need to be made, but you start to track your ratios - *the other numbers* - that comprise the sales funnel, with a view to making improvements at each defined stage of the sales process.

It is not good enough just to know how many calls it takes to get a meeting, but requires that we each know how efficient our calls are, and how to be ruthlessly efficient at each stage of the lifecycle of a given deal.

What makes this book different?

This book is not just about providing generic advice with limited direction. It is specifically focused on giving you the quickest and most effective methods of securing appointments and generating sales leads that ultimately generate revenue.

What is different about this book, is that it:

- Tells you what to do
- Shows you how to do it
- Provides tools to enable the creation of compelling propositions for any functional manager operating in any industry vertical
- Delivers scripts and sample language to facilitate you actually picking up the phone to call, and be successful
- Enables you to benchmark how you are performing and improving
- Shows you how to monitor progress to get the most out of each call
- Provides a comprehensive and unique system to maximise the results from every call that you make

I have deliberately used language that will be familiar to all sales people and provided templates of tools for you to use in support of your efforts. These tools will help you focus on your key objectives.

THE JOURNEY STARTS WITH SELF DISCOVERY

Identify suspects
↓
Build relevant and focussed value-propositions
↓
Secure appointments
↓
Convert them into qualified leads
↓
Close the sale
↓
Become a Sales Superstar

Do I need to read the entire book, cover to cover?

Not necessarily.

Firstly, if you're happy killing yourself making lots and lots of calls to get a single appointment and consequently failing to meet your sales targets each year, then don't read on – there is no shame in continuing to fail, you just lose your job!

Secondly, each of the chapters in this book stands alone, so that you can dip in and out of the book as necessary. Clearly, if you want to be a Sales Superstar, then you will dedicate a small amount of time each day to reading this book - it will make a substantial difference to your sales performance and radically alter your conversion rate leading ultimately to a positive effect on your bank account.

Think of that designer watch, fast car, palatial home or that luxury cruise. Follow the techniques in this book and turn your dreams into reality.

Once you have read this book and started to show progress, generate more meetings and close more sales, this book can be used as a reference guide to aid you in fine-tuning your excellence.

How long before I begin to see an improvement?

I cannot tell you exactly. But, if you are prepared to put all of this advice into practice and follow each of my steps in turn, then you will start to see results swiftly. The longer you delay, the longer it will be before you start to see improvement and start to achieve real success.

THE KEY IS TO START

Positive action will always generate a positive response. Guaranteed. If you don't start, how can you ultimately improve? So JUST DO IT.

CHAPTER 2

Defining what success looks like

Success means different things to different people, but if you are selling anything to anyone, then the chances are that you have a target that you measure success or failure against.

However, in my experience, many sales people almost go into a mild form of denial about their sales target and fail to either actually know what their target is, what progress they have made against delivering it on a daily basis, or know when the target has to be delivered so that they can have a celebration or "victory lap".

TASK 1

With specific reference to the page marked *My Sales Target,* (Page 12) complete a version of this sheet, with your particular details and name at the top, print it out and keep it available to refer to it every morning before you start to sell. It will help ensure you don't forget the task in hand

By completing this task, you are focusing explicitly on the sales target in your head, how much has to be delivered by when, and in doing so you are mentally committing to achieving that target and being successful. Knowing and buying into the target is the first step to sales success.

At this point I wanted to insert a note as I think it is really important to embrace success from the outset. Why the note at this point in the book? I believe that if you just shoot for 100% target achievement then you are not trying hard enough – Try to plan to achieve between 105 – 115% of your target, to guarantee you are successful and get paid really well at commission time.

TASK 2

Once you have clearly committed to your target (rather than just the target to get you to 100% achievement for your job), I find it useful to relate how my hard work will relate to the rewards that my success will bring me. If you haven't got a reward for yourself, then what is all the hard work for?

Complete the sheet entitled *Rewarding My Achievements* (Page 13), print a copy out and refer to it at the start of each week – cross off each item when you achieve it. Perhaps even have pictures of your dream house or whatever you are working towards, placed on your desk – having these visuals in front of you each day will help keep you motivated.

Focus and articulation on the target and subsequent reward, is critically important to the whole process, as it formulates a context for our behaviour. As humans, we are naturally conditioned to derive motivation from performing a task if we can see a form of reward at the end of it – rather like being a trained circus animal. So this process commits one to the target, and in turn provides motivation for activity and resulting achievement.

As part of my lead generation routine, I will make regular calls or perform regular research to start to become very specific about the item or event that is going to form my reward – colour, optional extras, ownership costs, delivery options, pricing and special offers etc. If you can mentally see yourself with that item, enjoying that pleasure or experiencing that reward, then it provides the psyche with the motivation to push through when times become tough or when success becomes limited – almost like a vision statement for the universe to hear, absorb and respond to.

COLD CALLS TO HOT LEADS

exercise

My Sales Target

I

_____
(Insert your name)

will generate

_____
(Insert revenue target)

in sales revenue for

_____
(Insert company name)

by

_____
(Insert date)

DEFINING WHAT SUCCESS LOOKS LIKE

exercise

Rewarding My Achievements

100% — When I have achieved 100% of my target, I will buy myself

80% — When I have achieved 80% of my target, I will buy myself

60% — When I have achieved 60% of my target, I will buy myself

40% — When I have achieved 40% of my target, I will buy myself

20% — When I have achieved 20% of my target, I will buy myself

CHAPTER 3

The first step on the path to excellence

The world is full of exceptional sales people who think that they can sell anything to anyone. The reality is that many people with an inflated sense of their own self-worth are plain ordinary and often struggle to make their sales targets. Great sales people constantly monitor how they are performing and look for ways to better each time – lots of small adjustments along the way, adds up to a major improvement in the end result.

Knowing where the problem exists is the first stage to understanding how to fix the problem.

No matter how successful you have been in selling, it is always imperative to start with a simple benchmark to find out how you are currently performing, what is working and what can be improved –

think of it as a form of health check for your activities, which will provide you a sense for how well you are performing.

It sounds ridiculous, I know, but *The Funnel of Truth* helps sales people to:

- Quantify their current performance – How well are they performing at the moment and what does all that hard work translate to at the end of the year.
- Show the gap to be filled - Demonstrates the size of the task ahead of them and what they need to change in order to be more successful in selling and ultimately more successful.
- Benchmark performance against their peers – Provide a peer-benchmark to motivate a team to improve their performance.

Refer to *The Funnel of Truth* at the end of this chapter, and spend some time researching the input statistics so that you can accurately complete the calculations. Locating some of these statistics may take time and may require you to go to many separate sources of information. It is worth persevering at this stage as this is one of the most valuable exercises you can do.

Start by having a look back on how well you did last year – even if it was at a different company or different product area. We are looking to do some basic analysis that will be beneficial in understanding how to maximise your results. Prior evidence of your performance is the best place to start so that we can all understand what is working and where there are areas to be improved. To complete the funnel, let's work from the bottom upwards.

1. Start with the target you actually achieved - Write that in Box 1 on the funnel and record what percentage you achieved against target (if you don't know these figures then you have serious problems!).

2. Moving up the funnel, check how many customer contracts or offers you were successful in winning to get you to that number. It is rare for anyone to win 100% of all deals they are shortlisted for. Write that value in Box 2.

3. Obviously, to win business, you have to bid or submit an offer for the business, so in Box 3 write the total number of bids issued or offers made to customers to buy your service. This can be painful, but is all part of the improvement process. This will show how many overall deals you were actively part of, where you won some and lost some.

4. Before you or your company is able to participate in a customer purchase, you need to have some form of positive contact with the customer or a customer meeting to make them aware of your product or service – how many new business meetings you had. Put the total number of customer meetings organised in Box 4. It is unlikely that this will be a precise number, but a reasonably close estimate will be sufficient.

5. Box 5 should contain the total number of suspects contacted to get to the revenue number in Box 1. Think of it as how many people did you email, call, contact, mail directly etc., in the hope that they would pay

THE FIRST STEP ON THE PATH TO EXCELLENCE

attention to what you communicated to them, and give business to you. For many of you this is a very large number so an overall approximation will be fine.

Completing this sheet will help quantify the size of the task ahead and the scale of the improvement you will be able to make. It is not a difficult issue to resolve, but is one that you need to see visually so that you can refer back to it in a few months' time and see how much you have improved.

It is likely that the ratio of customers contacted to appointments made is about 40:1 or greater. If your ratio is smaller than that, then it indicates that you need to focus your energies on the other ratios lower down the sales funnel and improve them – the numbers game in action once again!

Applying the knowledge learned here will make all of your ratios smaller and increase the efficiency with which a suspect is progressed through your sales process, to become a live prospect, to contracts and ultimately to revenue. In short, the more we pay attention to these ratios, the smaller the amount of work we have to do for maximum return!

Now that you have filled in the *Funnel of Truth*, we need to do some basic analysis to make sense of these figures. Have a look at the example of a services company that was really struggling; it provides some invaluable lessons that you should apply to your completed sales funnel.

If we look at the total revenue figure of $1.4m (Box 1), we can see that they signed 81 (Box 2) customers to get to that number. We can easily calculate that the average contract value (revenue figure/total number of contracts) = $17,284

However, to get these 81 customers to deliver that revenue, the company had to issue 394 bids. We can therefore calculate that the win-ratio of (bids submitted/ customers won) – 4.86:1 – not a bad ratio but something to be improved upon.

Moving further up the funnel one can see that the company had to meet 2281 customers to be in a position to tender for bids showing a ratio of customer meetings to bids submitted (meetings/ bids issued) = 5.79:1

To achieve that level of revenue the company had to contact 49270 customers – a massive undertaking. The contact to meetings ratio (number of customers contacted/ number of meetings held) = 21.6:1

At this stage it would be easy for me to provide guidance on what is a good conversion rate and what it not, but each industry, in each country operates conversion rates that are unique to that market – there is no overall target ratio – every business is different. The object of what we learn here is to be constantly improving our ratios at every stage of the lifecycle of an opportunity right through the sales funnel. Small corrections in what we do, when we do it and how it is done, will make a large difference in the end.

What if I don't have prior ratios to compare?

For those who are relatively new to the whole sales world, it is entirely understandable that you may not yet have any prior history and associated sales ratios. This doesn't means you are excluded from this program, but means we have to start with generic assumptions on benchmark ratios so that you can have some basis on which to qualify your performance and measured improvement.

With reference to the *Funnel of Truth* working from the bottom up, write in what your sales target for the year in Box 1 – this will be clear to you and readily available from your manager. Before completing Box 2, speak to colleagues and get a feel for what the average contract value is for the business you work for, and write this figure down on the side of the page.

Next in Box 2, using the average order value you have found out, calculate the number of deals you need to close in order to deliver that sales target, by dividing your sales target by the average order value.

To calculate the number of deals you need to be actively participating in, for an entry into Box 3, I would take the entry in Box 2 and multiply by 5 – this assumes that you have a win rate of 20%, or win 1 in every 5 deals you actively participate in – a solid win ratio.

To calculate the number of prospects you need have, multiply the entry in Box 3 by 10 and write that calculation in Box 4 – this assumes that you actively participate in 10% of all deals as a result of your calling.

At this point, anyone in sales will know that the assumptions and ratios are such that if you spend time really planning each call, then you will be able to easily improve on these ratios and deliver more deals for fewer calls and prospects – and that is what this book will help you do.

How will I know when I am improving?

Having completed the *Funnel of Truth* earlier, you should now be in a position to actually see how you are performing relative to your funnel. No matter what it demonstrates, this visual representation of performance provides a comprehensive benchmark against which progress can be monitored.

I use the *Funnel of Truth* for companies as well as for coaching individuals; it is worthwhile doing your own personal funnel for your department or business, to see how your own performance compares to others in your area – that way you can see if you are above or below the team average and ensure that you get to the top. It is guaranteed, that when you are winning the game and leading your department's performance, everyone will want to know what you did and how you did it.

To capture your sales ratios refer to the *My Sales Ratios* page and complete this with the ratios you derived from your sales funnel. This will show you exactly how you are performing. Note the date at the top of the page and fill in another copy of this sheet each month and then at the end of each quarter – file each of them and refer back to your previous quarter to see clear improvements. You will see improvements visually and this will motive you to drive on – rather like exercise and weight loss!

Knowing these ratios will help you focus. Write them down and keep them with you. We will revisit them once you have implemented what you have learned.

THE FIRST STEP ON THE PATH TO EXCELLENCE

exercise

The Funnel of Truth

# of customers contacted	Box 5	
# of sales appointments	Box 4	
# of bids issued	Box 3	
# of contracts issued	Box 2	
Revenue Target & %	Box 1	

exercise

Example: Services Company

# of customers contacted	Box 5	49270
# of sales appointments	Box 4	2281
# of bids issued	Box 3	394
# of contracts issued	Box 2	81
Revenue Delivered	Box 1	$1.4m

THE FIRST STEP ON THE PATH TO EXCELLENCE

exercise

My Sales Ratios

Refer back to *The Funnel of Truth* to calculate the ratios:

AVERAGE CONTRACT VALUE

Box 1/ Box 2 =

WIN RATIO

Box 3/ Box 2 =

ATTRACTIVENESS RATIO

Box 4/ Box 3 =

"EFFICIENCY" RATIO

Box 5/ Box 4 =

CHAPTER 4

Farming the most fertile soil

Successful sales people realize that the best way to ensure they are successful either in a new job, or in selling a new product, or promoting a new service, is to look to emulate the areas of success that other successful sales professionals have farmed – essentially adopting their blueprint for success and replicating it.

What successful sales professionals have at the core of their DNA is a deep understanding that the simplest way to be successful is to understand where other successful colleagues have had positive results, and emulated them. Simple.

If your marketing team is any good (that is if you have one), they may be in a position to help you with this information and perhaps have clear attributes that you can use: who the clients are, where they are located, their business type, revenue profile, contract value, title of the decision maker etc. In truth, you want as much information as you can get to segment and use. They might even have purchased a large list of data from which you can segment to derive a list of suspects.

But if they don't have this information then you will need to understand the "recipe" – i.e. the common characteristics of these customers and do your own legwork.

Have a look at the database of existing customers your employer keeps. The chances are that these customers are typical of the customers you need to go after. You may need to ask for permission to analyse this, but it is time well spent. If there are literally thousands of customers, analyse the top 100 customers ranked by revenue or profitability, to find common characteristics.

Establish their common characteristics, and complete the *Customer Recipe* on the next page, it will help you target the most fruitful customers. Each of these questions may require a little detective work, but it is worth spending the time to get this right – understand the industry segments that have generated most sales in the past as well as the characteristics of these companies – then replicate success.

Once you have a rough idea of the *Customer Recipe*, I'd recommend speaking with other successful sales people and ask if they think your research is roughly correct. They may brush you off and be reluctant to share what has made them successful but be persistent, professional and focused. Understanding this recipe is pure gold.

exercise

Customer Recipe

Top Industry Segments	1
	2
	3
Location(s)	
Number of Employees	
Turnover	$
Multiple Geographies ?	Yes / No
If yes, where ?	A
	B
	C
Economic Buyer Job Title(s)	

Determining other segments to target

It is unlikely that in your new role, you will be lucky enough to sell into the very same segment as an existing team member and you will therefore have to consider targeting other potential customers either in other territories (quite likely) or other vertical markets.

Knowing who to contact, what to say and what will motivate them to continue a dialogue with you, is difficult at best, but following a few simple steps in this next section of the book will help you become successful and focused on speaking to these new suspects in a language they will likely respond to.

This process of focus requires a modular approach that, once completed, will provide an ongoing source of potential suspects for you to target and continue to build your pipeline.

Initially, one needs to determine those vertical markets (think industry verticals e.g. healthcare, education, finance etc.) that are likely to be receptive to your company's product or service i.e. could companies in these segments buy what you are offering. I frequently hear companies tell me that there are no limits to who can buy their product and whilst that may be technically true, few organisations have the scale and reach to establish a meaningful dialogue with lots of different industry verticals. In my experience a maximum of 10 industry verticals is optimal.

With specific reference to the *Industry Verticals* sheet at the end of this chapter, consider the product or service your company wants you to sell, and in less than 2 minutes, write down all those industry vertical markets in the boxes provided, where you *could* conceivably be successful in selling what you offer. Once completed, I would sit with a colleague to validate that these 10 segments are realistic potential target segments. Update and change the contents of the sheet with any comments until you have a robust sheet with 10 potential industry verticals.

With the list of target verticals in the *Industry Verticals* sheet now created, you should prioritise this list to determine those verticals which will provide the best and most profitable results, quickest. I usually try to seek advice from colleagues, friends and industry acquaintances to determine priority verticals. To ensure that you are focussing your energy in a key segment where there is money available, I usually cross-reference the industry vertical research with any external industry research to determine market value and size. Add this information to the *Industry Verticals* sheet next to each segment's entry.

Having collated this information, you are now in a position to determine the priority of any new target verticals. Referring to the *Industry Verticals* sheet, prioritise these key verticals 1 through 10. In a different coloured pen, circle the top 3 vertical segments and prioritise these as the key focus.

Now refer back to the *Customer Recipe*, completed previously, and overlay these top 3 industry verticals – you now have not only a prioritised list of key verticals to target, but also the key attributes of the companies where you or your company have had the most appropriate success. There is a small chance that the *Customer Recipe* may not necessarily translate across Industry vertical segments, but using what you know works, is a logical place to start your journey to farming the most fertile soil for leads and deals.

FARMING THE MOST FERTILE SOIL

exercise

Industry Verticals

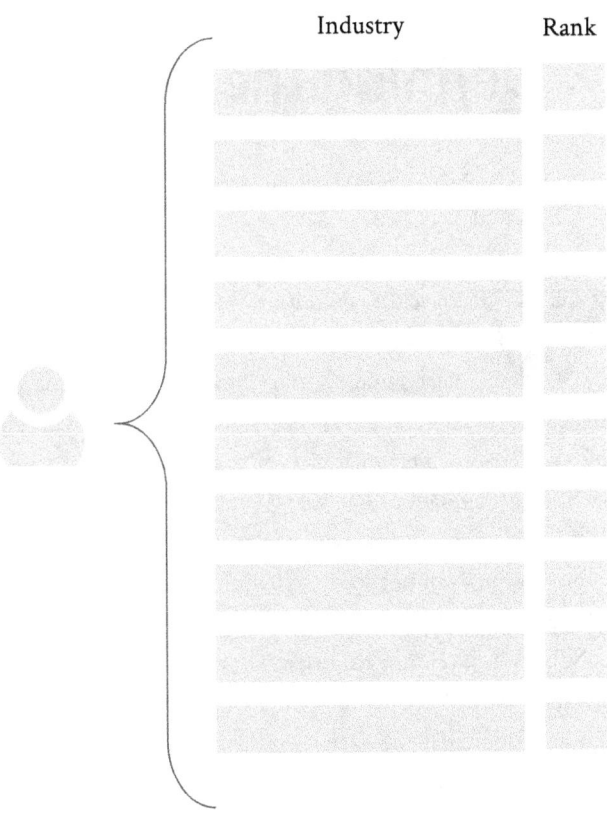

CHAPTER 4

Defining the universe

With clear definition of the Customer Recipe and Industry Verticals, you are now in great shape to start building your "universe" of suspects to target. This can be a very complex process unless you have completed your *Customer Recipe* which will help you formulate market segmentation, but having completed that work I favour an approach that blends previous contacts (people who you may have met in a previous role, are professional connections etc.) with newly acquired contacts from a range of sources.

Why? It is easier to reach your sales target if you contact customers who have either bought from you previously or those who exactly match the recipe you derived earlier – in short, I am trying to make your life easier!

To get that list of potential customers, you need to go after several different segments to maximize the chances of creating a large enough and fertile enough universe of suspects.

EXISTING CUSTOMERS

My favorite target segment is those customers that have already bought from you (either in your present role or in a past life) or the company you are working for. They will have overcome the familiarization with you or your company, and provided the previous service was acceptable, will be receptive to buying from you again.

AN UPSELL IS EASIER THAN A NEW SELL

On average 30% of all existing customers will have a change of personnel each year – so about 1:3 of all existing customers are ready to be re-sold each year and are re-familiarized with your products and new services so you always have existing contacts or companies to consider as an initial universe to attack.

A good idea is to go back to existing customers or existing contacts, and provided there have been no account or personal issues, contact those companies to be both a courteous account manager, but to also see what else can be sold to them.

TRADE DIRECTORIES OF COMMUNITIES OF INTEREST

This is an age-old area that is often used for building a customer list, but still beneficial.

There are many trade bodies that represent industries in many different countries. Usually, these trade bodies have good websites and provide comprehensive list of all their members, with contact details – exactly what you need to get started. If you can get a list of the members of these trade bodies, then these are a perfect addition to your customer "universe". Where possible add members of 2 trade bodies to your list of potential suspects – once you start to call a vertical, you are refining your pitch again and again – each time becoming more and more proficient and honed in your communications.

GENERAL MARKET DATA – A "SOLAR SYSTEM"

You may find that the most productive segment for you to target is one that does not seem to have a Trade Association of readily identifiable community of any kind. In this instance, you are going to have to define the "Solar System" (a smaller part of a universe), yourself. This is one of the hardest parts of the entire exercise. I find there are 3 potential sources for this data:

1. Build the list of data from publicly available sources using the internet, industry journals, closed user groups – this is time consuming and can be counter-productive but will provide some data for you to use.

2. Purchase the data from the array of data and list brokers. If the marketing folk know anything about your target customer segments, they should be able to help. Otherwise you should be in good shape to tell the data company your ideal customer profile – you have already done the Customer Recipe, which you can send to them directly. They will then be able to do a match against their data universe to provide you with an accurate set of new customers. It is worth noting that you need to be absolutely sure you are legally able to call the list provided and you need to remember that typically, this list is provided to you on a "rental" basis – so you need to use it as the basis for your calling so that you can build on the data provided.

3. LinkedIn – Now an essential part of the commercial landscape, LinkedIn provides invaluable help in identifying key personnel, companies and areas to explore. I find that time spent here can help you build out your data universe to add key contacts, their name, their past employment history, related companies that they may work with and potential other avenues of interest.

If you are starting a new business and do not have the funds to buy data, then using LinkedIn to start to identify and target your universe of potential suspects is really the most efficient and cost effective manner to identify the Solar System you are targeting. It does take time, but time spent here, will guarantee more efficient results and a fast target attainment – so do this step carefully. This data will be an investment and provided you have the *Customer Recipe* correct, you'll be in good shape to get exactly the right data to start.

> **TIP:**
> A note of caution before you rush off and buy data – it is only useful if you can use it. By that, I mean, it is only of use if you can call the list in time. Many companies never actually use it in a timely manner, so by the time they call, as much as 60% of all the data can be outdated and is therefore wasted.

In short, you only need to build a Solar System of data to keep you calling for the next 90 days – so take the calculations derived from the *Funnel of Truth*, and divide by 4 – this gives you a rough approximation of what you need to do in the next 90 days. Any data that is more than 6 months old, will have degraded to such an extent that it is worthless - just compile what you need in the short term and no more – anything else will be wasted at this stage.

Competitor customers

Depending on your level of confidence, it can be useful to target the customers signed by your competitors. We have all seen it, the press release that tells of a deal won, maybe the value of the deal, what was sold and where it was deployed – but what many people fail to recognise, is that this identifies a customer who has requirements for services like yours, and may need more next year. Sometimes you get lucky and the press release identifies the length of the contract – so you know when it will be up for review and you will be able to call to participate in the buying cycle next time around.

Diarise this information 3-6 months before the contract is due to expire and be prepared to nurture the prospect, so that you are in a position to bid when the tender is up again. It is worth regularly checking the websites of competitors and compiling a list of their customers. You never know when these customers may be grateful to hear from a friendly voice and this ensures that not only are you focussing on your own success, but you are keeping a watching eye on market developments and may learn a new tactic to be successful that others are using and you haven't yet learned.

Data, data everywhere, but where do I start?

Some sales people will stick to a single group of suspects, I prefer to target a mixture of suspects – this provides variety to my calling, and enables me to be sure that I am not wasting my time, calling unproductive clients.

By now you probably have a large universe of suspects just ready to receive your calls. But with a task of this kind, much like eating elephants, it needs to be tackled a piece at a time. So collate all the data in your data sheet. This will provide manageable chunks of data to contact and ensure valuable pieces of information gleaned when calling, are recorded somewhere, even if you do not have a CRM system.

Now you need to do some manual sifting to eliminate duplicate records – I suggest re-ordering your list alphabetically, this will throw up duplicates enabling you to delete them and produce an effective target list. With a de-duplicated list, now is the time to start focussing on prioritising your calls.

Divide the list of suspects into 100 record chunks – this is not such a large universe that it becomes unmanageable, but is large enough to give you plenty of suspects to call in a reasonable timeframe. It is also small enough that you will not be daunted by the task at hand and can swiftly see progress being made.

So, section off the top 100 records. Call this Batch 1. Do the same with the rest of the records, dividing them into equally-sized batches until all the records have been put into batches. If you are dealing with a much larger universe of suspects and your calling rate is extremely high each day, I suggest making these batches larger, but not so large that the task appears daunting or just too big to be successful at – smaller batches are better.

Now you have successfully defined who you are going to target and derived a list of suspects to be contacted, you are in a position to start calling.

TO DO

- ☐ Compile your sales numbers for last year
- ☐ Complete the *Funnel Of Truth*
- ☐ Complete *My Sales Ratios* sheet
- ☐ Analyse existing customer list and complete *Customer Recipe*
- ☐ Speak to lead sales person to confirm *Customer Recipe* is correct
- ☐ Confirm generic customer recipe with marketing staff
- ☐ Produce list of Top 10 potential industry verticals, and prioritise attack
- ☐ Collate all data in a single sheet ready to contact for sales
- ☐ Add list of existing customers to contact
- ☐ Add members of 2 trade directories
- ☐ Add "Solar System" data
- ☐ Add competitor customers
- ☐ Re-order all data alphabetically
- ☐ Sift-out duplicate records to leave you with single list of suspects
- ☐ Divide up the data into manageable batches of 100 records

CHAPTER 5

The first step to success – starting!

This is where we put all of our planning, research and homework into action and focus on generating revenue to start delivering results and *Reward Your (My) Achievements* – refer back to the completed sheet at the end of Chapter 2 and see what you are working towards. Visualise the items, feel them in your mind and they will be yours. I often advise people to pin this list to their desk and refer to it each day – it maintains focus, generates momentum and stimulates lively internal debate amongst colleagues, whilst also acting as a key focal point when times are tough.

You should now have a fairly large amount of data and are ready to start calling but where to start? We will start by taking all the records in Batch 1 and begin with these.

THE FIRST STEP TO SUCCESS - STARTING!

Each person will have a different target number of calls to make to reach their sales target (you will know this number now that you have completed the *Funnel of Truth*), but for simplicity's sake assume you will need to make 10 calls each day to generate 1 new business appointment.

A batch of 100 records should therefore keep you going for 2 weeks (10 calls per day x 10 working days), meaning that you are calling about 2400 suspects per year. Again, calculate your ratios and refer back to the ratios sheet earlier to see if you need to call more or fewer and adjust your daily calling volumes accordingly.

I have a basic strategy that I suggest you adopt. Let us assume that your ratio analysis indicates that to reach your revenue target this year, you need to call on 2400 customers? Never assume that this is an exact science, and with everything you do, always plan to exceed your revenue target early in the year – so add a further 10% to that calling number – so you need to call 2680 suspects not 2400.

Given that revenue is cumulatively added to your total, the earlier you call these customers, the more chance you have of reaching your target. So when I am starting the program, I usually like to start by calling double the number of suspects I need to call so that I am accelerating my performance and success early.

*CALL MORE SUSPECTS THAN YOU NEED TO;
AND CALL THEM AS SOON AS YOU CAN.*

Take that number of suspects to be called, and divide it by 45 (the number of available working weeks assuming holidays and holiday seasons).

Now you have the total number of weekly suspects you need to call, divide this by 5 to give you a daily call target.

In the example above:
- 2680 prospects
- About 60 calls per week (45 week year)
- Or 12 calls per day

Before you pick up the phone and start on the path to sales excellence, go back and review *Rewarding My Achievements* at the end of Chapter 2 - the reason you are doing this - and understand how many calls you are going to have to make, to successfully deliver your target. Once you understand exactly why you are doing this, you are in the best position to start putting theory into practice.

Divide up the total number of calls to be made, so that you have an equal number of prospecting calls each day. This daily discipline ensures you are always generating new customer opportunities and constantly topping up your sales funnel – ceasing to call can often result in a reduced sales pipeline and reduced commission, and we don't want that.

Refer to Batch 1 in your calling list. I suggest you break those records into small segments – perhaps colour code them – so you can easily see how many need to be called each day. Your calling schedule should look like this:

Day 1	Clean the data & research companies to call on Day 2
Day 2	Call and set appointments with all data cleaned on Day 1, clean and research new data for Day 3 calling
Day 3	Call and set appointments with all data cleaned on Day 2, clean and research new data for Day 4 calling
Day 4	Call and set appointments with all data cleaned on Day 3, clean and research new data for Day 5 calling
Day 5	Call and set appointments with all data cleaned on Day 4, clean and research new data for Day 6 calling. Collate weekly progress sheet.

Cleaning the data

You will see from the weekly schedule above, that I have outlined 2 distinct tasks that will make a huge difference to your calls to appointments ratio. Firstly, before you call any decision-maker, you must confirm that they are:

a. The most appropriate person to take your sales call, and if they are not then find out who is
b. Located at the office you think they're at, and if not find out where they are
c. Still do that job, and if not, correctly identify who is

It makes your job easier if you are calling the right person at the right location!

Making that first call is the first call on your path to sales success, but you need to start first! With your calling sheet in front of you, start calling the companies in Batch 1 to verify the accuracy of the data you compiled above.

I adopt a relaxed style when making this call. To make your job easier, here is a simple script that I have developed (Page 46).

This is a very quick call (typically less than 20 seconds) and will mean that you not only have the right contact, but you have broken that mental barrier to calling that company – the next call you to that contact, will feel less like a cold call and the barrier of calling has already been removed. Verifying details first not only ensures you are calling the correct contact, but reduces some of the mental barriers associated with calling net new contacts.

What if the company has a no-names policy?

This is increasingly common and makes life tough, but there are several ways around this.

What I usually do is phone the company back after a while, so that the receptionist forgets the sounds of your voice and thinks you are another random caller, and ask to be put through to the IT department. When they answer the phone I sigh, informing the respondent that the switchboard operator has put me through to the wrong person and ask them to transfer me to the relevant decision-maker. They usually do this without thought and before they do you politely ask, "Can you just confirm their name and their secretary's name please?" – You are in! You will see a sample script for this call later.

If you cannot get a name using my tip above then there is no substitute for trawling LinkedIn and finding the correct contact by searching on the company name and then identifying the correct functional manager. When phoning back, you are then in a position to ask to speak to the correct person. This now completes the strategy and planning associated with defining who to call and how to plan the calling work.

Why do they keep saying "No"?

As you participate in this program and start generating strong leads and sales success, you will inevitably come across suspects that will say "No" to what you are proposing. This is to be expected and not something within your control.

All too often, when you get a "No" from a suspect, at its core, they are telling you that they are inherently happy with the status quo and want things to stay the way they are currently. The old phrase "If it isn't broken, then don't fix it" resonates with lots of people that say no to your proposal.

There will be a myriad of reasons for the negative response – maybe peer pressure, prior experience, lack of understanding, disbelief, cultural reasons, maybe racial barriers – all of which are outside your control and may be significant contributors to the "No". These are variables outside your control, and will sometimes make you feel a little deflated and questioning what you are doing and how you are doing it.

What is worth considering is the fact that the status quo never remains the same – the status quo is a current state and in no way reflective of the way things *will be* in the future. Where would the world be without the Internet and remaining steadfastly embracing paper only? Or where would we be if humanity had not embraced the car and remained with the horse as the primary mode of transport? Consider this when you reach a no and remember that an ability to portray how your product or service could be pivotal for the future of a suspect's business, is a critical part of refining and delivering your pitch.

Just one more piece of homework

Now that you know the exact person you are going to be calling, it is important you have some idea about their business.

For each of the companies you are going to call, go onto their website and write on the call sheet, 3 pieces of information about the company – e.g. recent company news, a customer success, new executive appointment. For large companies where there is a lot of information or companies where there is a lot of detail that will be of value to you in supporting your sale, I usually like to print out this info and collate it with the call sheet, so that I have specific info to refer to when I am on the phone. It demonstrates professionalism to the process.

Gaining some knowledge about the company you are calling will put you head and shoulders over your competition. Your knowledge will also enable you to fully understand how your product or service might be of benefit to them - you will start to focus on delivering a proposition specifically for them. Additionally, it identifies to the caller that you are not some random "Smile and Dial" sales person who is hoping to get lucky – you have researched your call with background information and have taken time to learn how to be relevant.

Now you are really making progress.

THE FIRST STEP TO SUCCESS - STARTING!

TO DO

- ☐ Refer back to the *Rewarding My Achievements* and your *Sales Target* sheet to remind yourself why you are doing this
- ☐ Calculate the number of suspects you need to call, on the basis of your ratios (see Chapter 2) – write this number at the top of your calling sheet
- ☐ Add 10% to the number of suspects you need to call
- ☐ Divide this number by 45 (assuming some holiday each year and fewer calls over holiday periods) to give you a weekly call total
- ☐ Divide this by 5 to give a daily call target
- ☐ Phone daily to verify correct decision-maker contact details, for calling the following day
- ☐ Collate at least 3 pieces of company information for each company you intend to call
- ☐ Note all information on a calling sheet

script

Data Verification Call

"Hi, this is _____ from _____
           (Insert your name)   (Insert your company's name)

and I am just phoning to check that _____
                               (Insert business contact's name)

is still the _____ for your company, and is
        (Insert job title)

located at _____ ".
       (Insert company address)

Await response....

If yes, then:

Thank you. (end call)

If no, then:

Please could you give me the name of their replacement/ new location? (note down information on calling sheet and end call)

script

No Names Policy

Use this script if you have tried to verify the contact name, but the operator has told you that the company operates a no-names policy.

In a relaxed voice only .....

"Hi, can you put me through to the guys in IT please?"

Await response once transferred:

"Hi, is that _____ office?"
         (Insert contacts name)

Typical answer – "No"

"Sorry, I was trying to get through to _____
                                         (Insert contacts name)
office.   Is he/she still there?"

Await response. Note down either new name or location.

"Can you transfer me please or give me their direct line?"

(Take notes and add these to your calling sheet)

CHAPTER 6

Planning your pitch

With a detailed knowledge of the universe of suspects you are now going to target, the correct decision-maker within each company and some background information, you are now in excellent shape to start calling suspects and setting appointments for them to start buying from you.

Before you can actually start to successfully set appointments, you need to do some practicing and consider some crucial, often unwritten, areas that will massively influence your chances of success.

Whenever any of us responds to a call, we instinctively react to the mood projected by the caller – so if the caller sounds miserable or tired, then we react accordingly. If they sound happy and positive then we respond in the same way – so we want to project a positive attitude, so that what we say is met with a positive response.

There are several things you can do when calling:

- Make all of these calls whilst <u>standing up</u> – this increases circulation, generates a degree of vibrancy and urgency in your voice.
- <u>Smile</u> – if you smile when you talk, the person on the other end of the phone will detect this and respond positively – practice making calls by looking in a mirror – it's a good way to make certain you are smiling so go and buy one now!

A good hint that's served me well is to stand up and make the calls – this regulates your breathing, puts you in a strong frame of mind and makes your voice sound positive – it makes a real difference. Try to use a headset rather than a handset to make that call as you will probably find that you use your hands to express yourself and are freer – again, it will come through in your voice, intonation and mood and we almost always "talk" with our hands.

The most effective time to call

I advise all my clients to encourage sales people to get into the office early – before the conventional start of the business day – at about 08:00 – 08:15. This time is sometimes referred to as the "Golden Hour" and is typically the most productive hour of any business day for many staff.

The simple logic is that any decision-maker that you want to target, probably has a secretary or "gatekeeper", who will start work at conventional office times (09:00 – 18:00), so calling before this person starts work, it's more likely to get you straight through to the decision-maker than calling when your competitors start calling, say mid-morning after their coffee and breakfast.

The highest performing sales-people I have come across (and therefore people we should try to emulate) get in early when their own office is relatively quiet. They make their appointment-setting calls before the majority of their office has arrived (and kept their scripts and sales techniques secret), avoiding any background noise or distractions. Having completed their daily call routines, they are effectively beginning that conventional business day knowing that they have done their calling quota whilst they are fresh and filled their sales funnel for guaranteed success.

Whilst I have made mention of the Golden Hour as the optimum time to call and speak with any decision-maker, there is an additional timeslot when it is very likely that you will be able to speak to the same decision-maker - what I call the "Silver Hour" – not as precious as the first quiet hour of the working day, but this hour is also likely to be good for calling.

The Silver hour is from 5.45-6.45pm, after the time when the "gatekeeper" has gone home, and when the decision-maker is still likely to be in the office. There is a chance that the decision-maker will be in the office and receptive to your call but you run the risk of missing them at the end of the day.

Super-successful sales professionals like to complete their quota of daily calls early, so doing an extra 1 or 2 calls daily is the same as adding 300-500 calls per year – which can make a big difference in sales revenue!

Knowing what to say when you do get through

There are 5 elements that are essential if your cold-call is going to generate results:

- a. Grab their attention
- b. Identify yourself and your company
- c. Tell them why you are calling them
- d. Ask a question to qualify them and demonstrate knowledge
- e. Answer the unwritten question, "Why bother speaking to me?"
- f. Ask for the appointment, suggesting a time, date and their office

GRAB THEIR ATTENTION

Starting the conversation is often the hardest part. All too often sales people start with an opening that is just a gimmick, the classic line, "If I could save you X, would you be interested?" - IT HAS A LOW CHANCE OF SUCCESS. Ask a sensible question or make a reasonable statement and you will get a reasonable answer.

The easiest way for any sales person to grab the attention of the person on the other end of the telephone is to say their name:

"Good Morning Mr. Smith".

They have been called that their whole life and if their name is called out in a crowded room, they are likely to respond to it - So use their name. The aim here is to start generating positive momentum in the conversation with Mr Smith, and ensure that he responds positively to you – it makes it harder for them to say "No", when you request that appointment.

Remember, the key thing here is to get a response (be it a silent agreement, acknowledgement that their name really is Smith or even a hang-up).

IDENTIFY YOURSELF AND YOUR COMPANY

Once you have greeted the caller, you need to identify yourself and your company. A simple approach is best here,

> *"Good Morning Mr. Smith, this is Nick Jones from Nick Jones Corp, we are a specialist flooring company based in London, with offices across the UK".*

We identify ourselves personally and introduce the company with a small company advert or commercial – a 1-sentence description of who the company is. The chances are that they have never heard of you, so you need to make some qualification of why you are calling.

TELL THEM WHY YOU ARE CALLING THEM

You are not calling them for a social chat, but you want to meet them to sell them something. Again, I favour a direct and uncomplicated approach:

> *"I am calling today to set up an appointment with you"*

If you give them no idea why you are calling, what are they supposed to say? Tell them why you are calling and you stand a real chance that they are going to say yes to meeting you. This is really important to anyone wanting to be better at cold-calling and appointment setting. You are calling to set an appointment, nothing more.

ASK A QUESTION TO QUALIFY THEM AND DEMONSTRATE KNOWLEDGE

Adding a comment or question to qualify the company is a good way of demonstrating knowledge (remember you did the research of the 3 key company facts before?), but it also provides an opportunity for the respondent to answer positively – which is what you want!

Do not ask open-ended questions, where the answer could be either a Yes or a No – as you will limit the potentially positive response rate to 50%!

The best way to do this is to ask a closed question after a statement, like,

> *"Mr. Smith, I note from your website that you have recently expanded operations to include a new manufacturing plant in Germany, and I'm sure that like Company A (a company he will have heard of and be flattered being compared to) you will be interested in development programs specifically targeting the German-speaking market?"*

This line of statement (proven knowledge) and closed question is more than likely going to provide you with a "Yes".

ANSWER THE UNWRITTEN QUESTION: "WHAT IS IN IT FOR THE PROSPECT?"

Often referred to as the Value Proposition, this is core the success or failure of your call.

There are thousands of text books devoted to articulating your "elevator pitch" both in terms of your company and the specific product or service you are selling and how it might relate to a given market. Getting this right virtually guarantees you success in securing the next conversation with the suspect you have called.

It is critically important to get this right. The first step is to think about one or two things that you believe your customers will positively respond to and that you personally believe in. Look for ways to communicate those ideas simply and succinctly. Use whatever experience you have from previous correspondence to executives, for guidance on how to structure conversations with them. Ask colleagues who are successful to perhaps provide guidance and don't feel afraid to ask for help from anyone else that has a customer-facing role like your own. Odds are that they have wrestled with the same issue and will have some help to offer.

An elevator pitch should always conclude with a call to action which will vary depending on the person you are talking to – and should involve, almost always, a meeting request or an agreement to a further conversation and move matters down the sales funnel.

Once you have crafted a sales pitch, try it out with a colleague in the same way that you have practiced the various scripts you have crafted. All of the work in creating a pitch will be wasted unless you prepare the delivery of that message whenever you need to.

For example:

"Wal-Mart – Everyday low prices"

> *"Company X will realize <quantified business enhancement> by purchasing <your service/ product> for <insert price/ cost>.*
>
> *Beginning <insert start date>, our product/ service will improve <insert specific function> and achieve a payback in <insert time frame>"*

As technical as the above example is, it is useful in demonstrating several key elements of the pitch that you will need to prepare for your prospects – talks about savings and associated improvements in business performance.

Almost all business purchasing decisions will be motivated by several key criteria – cost savings, increasing revenue, increasing customer loyalty and retention, and building real competitive market advantage – the focus is on essential business enhancing purchases. What you are trying to get the prospect to consider purchasing needs to fall into one of these key areas or it is likely that you will fall at the first hurdle and not get a meeting at all.

Before you pick up the phone you need to have articulated the value that your product or service delivers for the company you are calling, and have some idea of verifiable and quantifiable value – what you product does and how it will improve the suspect's business.

I create my value propositions in a simple way:

- Key product value delivered (not the product featured, but what business benefit they can measure and is delivered).

- Quantify the benefits, and where possible, refer to a brand-customer that has deployed what you are selling and the quantifiable benefit derived.
- If the customer purchases now, provide some indication of when they will realize that benefit.

Now that you have the overall value-proposition for what you are selling and how it will materially improve the lives of those that purchase or use it, you can now create a value-proposition that is tailored for 3 of the key decision-makers that you will need to influence as you move closer to closing the sale.

Tailoring the message for different audiences

The Value Proposition you create for the company you are calling, will clearly provide the suspect with a high-level overview of the quantifiable benefits they will derive from what you have to sell. But before you can successfully celebrate a win, you will likely have to convince several different types of functional manager along the way, each of whom has a different perspective on what they consider important.

If you think about your own organization, what might be important to your finance department – e.g. cost control, maximizing profitability and revenue - may be different from your HR department who may be more interested about, for example, staff retention rates, the pace of staff recruitment and performance monitoring. What is key, is that you recognize that within an organization you will probably need to sell to several functional managers and your message will need to be tailored so that they understand what you will be doing to help them.

Refer to the *Tailoring the Message* sheet at the end of this chapter. Create 3 copies of this and complete a sheet for each of the key functional managers that you are likely to have to speak with as you move to closing the deal. This research to understand their motivations, drivers and what keeps them awake at night, will help you tailor detailed elements of what you have to offer in a focused manner so that when you do deliver your pitch to them, it will be in a language that they understand and address some of their key drivers.

Ask for that appointment

This is now the easy bit, but for so many sales people, they get it wrong and it actually turns into the hardest bit for them. Provided you have articulated the value of what you are selling (tailored according to the suspect's functional needs) and the prospect is vaguely interested, you simply need to ask for the appointment. For example "That is great Mr. Smith, why don't we meet up next Wednesday at 4pm. I will come to your office. OK?"

The best approach here is to be brief, specific, polite and direct. Again, your language should move the discussion on from actually agreeing to the meeting, to when the best time would be to have the meeting – you have closed on the meeting and now it is just a matter of logistics. This is a simple assumptive close and highly effective – you remove doubt from the equation and move straight to certainty.

Ask and you will get – failure to ask for the meeting, will NOT get you the meeting.

A quick note about choosing the time of that meeting – I usually chose a Tuesday or Thursday morning and chose that day about 3-4 weeks out – the chances are that the diary won't be so full that far out and a Tuesday or Thursday are days that are traditionally less busy.

Practice, Practice, Practice

Before I make a single call to a suspect, I validate what I am proposing to say with a colleague to get their feedback. They will usually provide unbiased and very direct feedback about how good (or bad) your pitch is and help provide you some pointers on what needs to be refined. Take their feedback on board, and refine until the pitch is as sharp as it can be.

Once you are comfortable with your pitch, go home and standing in front of the mirror smiling, deliver your pitch at least 5 times. This will make you feel comfortable in saying what you have to say and you will further refine the language and delivery so that it is near perfect – you are now ready to start pitching for meetings.

TO DO

- ☐ Refer to the sample scripts and start to draft your particular scripts for calling
- ☐ Spend time refining your "Why me" statement or value proposition at a high level
- ☐ Identify the top 3 functional managers you will need to involve/ sell to as part of securing that sale
- ☐ Create a specific value-proposition for your product or service, tailored to each of them
- ☐ Validate your script and approach with colleagues to refine the approach
- ☐ Buy a mirror and practice your scripts whilst looking into it, smiling
- ☐ Practice your script 5 times before making a single call
- ☐ Make the first call
- ☐ Review how it went and make changes for the second call
- ☐ Do it again and keep going!

exercise

Tailoring the message

Functional Manager Name

Job Title

Department

Their main business drivers or issues

1.

2.

3.

How what you are selling addresses their drivers/ issues

1.

2.

3.

PLANNING YOUR PITCH

script

3rd Party Endorsement

Use this script if you have had some particular success in a sector or industry and want to leverage that success to secure more meetings with other companies in that sector.

In a relaxed voice only .....

Good morning _____ this is, _____
                        (Insert business contact's name)   (Insert your name)

from _____ . The reason that I am calling today
      (Insert company)

is that we have just finished doing some work for

_____ that generated excellent
(Insert name of company in their sector, that they will know)

results by _____
           (Insert examples of value added, costs reduced etc)

What I would like to do is to come and see you to talk through

the success we had at _____ and how we might
                              (Insert Company)

be able to generate similar success for you. How does

_____ sound?
(Suggest date & time)

script

Referral

Use this script if you have tried to set an appointment with another contact but been unsuccessful, BUT they have suggested that somebody else is a more appropriate contact.

In a relaxed voice only .....

Good morning _____ , this is _____
(Insert contact's name) (Insert your name)

from _____ .
(Insert company name)

The reason I am calling today is that we have been speaking

to _____ and they suggested that I give you a call
(Insert name of contact that referred you)

to arrange a meeting. I was wondering if _____
(Suggest date & time)

would work for you?

script

Follow Up

Use this script if you have tried to set an appointment with somebody who has suggested that you call them back later to arrange and appointment.

In a relaxed voice only .....

Good morning _____ , this is _____
                      (Insert contact's name)   (Insert your name)

from _____ .
      (Insert company name)

A number of weeks ago I contacted you and you indicated that I

should call you back to arrange a convenient time to call.

Would _____ work for you?
        (Suggest date & time)

CHAPTER 6

Success starts now

Having spent valuable time understanding your target audience, refining the message you are planning on delivering to them and the key parts of the conversation, you are now ready to start taking action. The key for success is actually committing, so you need to start immediately – today, now.

The key in securing a meeting with the decision-makers is to plan, execute and keep executing and refining as you go – there is no substitute for hard work. This will slowly build new sales appointments and general new sales, but only after the hard work has been done.

You will eventually stop needing to refer to these scripts and information you prepared in Chapters 4 & 5, but they are useful in making you more comfortable with calling – in time these will become automatic and you will refine them mid-conversation according to the flow, any objections and any areas of interest.

Making the call

Making your first call will be the hardest part. It may not go perfectly to plan, you may not speak to a decision-maker, or may result in a rejection, but with planning and purpose you will triumph and be successful.

When you are ready to start, I suggest you get into the office early during the Golden Hour (and before everybody else is around you), get your scripts out for easy reference and dial the first number on the call data sheet. This is the moment of commitment but the critical part if you are to be the best sales person.

No matter whether you manage to speak to the contact or not, you have started and broken the mystique surrounding calling people who may not know you. Every call you make from now onwards, will be an easier call to make and you will definitely speak to potential customers and win more deals. You have started on the path to success.

At this point I want to acknowledge that you will almost certainly make mistakes, lots of them and that is perfectly normal. You are starting something afresh, something you may not necessarily have all the skills in being expert at, so making errors & mistakes is perfectly natural. In fact, if you make no errors, then there is a case to say that maybe you are not trying hard or just plain lying to yourself. The best thing we can all do when we make a mistake is not to dwell on it – it happens and is a fundamental building block of the corporate characteristics that we all seek to accumulate lots of – experience. No mistakes, means you have diminished experience, more mistakes means you know what to avoid, what doesn't work and are what other paths might be open to success.

When you make a mistake, there is a clear lesson to be learned. Immediately following the call, write down precisely what happened, where the call went wrong and spend time understanding what you could have done differently – language used, tone, speed of voice, message, call-to-action? Analyse each of these areas and use this info to update or inform your script. Incorporating these learnings into your scripts will make them better still.

By actually making the calls, you are getting it right. You have committed to calling, learning and refining which puts you miles ahead of other sales professionals who aren't as committed to this course of action as you might be.

Communication in action

The temptation, once you actually have the suspect on the phone, is to talk faster, rush what you need to say and sound as though you have run a marathon and this is the first thing you are doing, having crossed the finish line. It is a natural reaction to a release of adrenaline at this stage, but you need to manage this temptation.

There is no doubting that a degree of enthusiasm projected down the phone will make the caller more interested in what you have to say, but in order to make sure they can clearly hear what you have to say, you need to concentrate on several key things that will have an immediate effect:

- Regulate your breathing – Ensure that you are breathing slowly and in a controlled manner, rather than rushing each breath.
- Concentrate on talking noticeably slower – Make a conscious effort to reduce the speed in which you speak

each word and focus on making each word clear to the listener.
- Lower the pitch and tone – When we become excited, many of us not only increase the speed with which we speak, but increase the tone and pitch so that our voices sound a few tones higher. When talking, take a softer and lower tone than we think we need to.

If you can focus on deliberately slowing your language, reducing the tone and sounding more precise on the call, then the caller will not be scared off from what you have to say, but will be in a position to actually hear your message, thereby increasing your chances of securing that next encounter.

Timing the call

There is no exact science that tells you each call will take a given number of minutes, and any longer or shorter than that and the call is not successful and failed to achieve its objective. I tend to find that if you have done your research and are clear with what you are asking, a successful call (where the reason for calling is clearly focussed on securing a meeting rather than a social call), will last between 2-3 minutes.

However, there are instances when a call may take longer – this is no bad thing. If the prospect (they have moved from suspect as you have them on the phone, have established dialogue and are qualifying them) is interested enough to spend time questioning you about what you are offering, then you should obviously spend as long as is necessary to demonstrate credibility – remember to use examples, demonstrate industry and sector knowledge, whilst asking questions to deduce key buying motivators. This is your moment to shine, so cutting the call short is not a good thing. A fluid dialogue is precisely what you are seeking to achieve when meeting, so why not start that dialogue early and build rapport when you get a chance.

"No" or "Send me more information"

Chances are that you will come across suspects that are not available when you call them. You need to keep these suspects as "still to be called" and include them in your next batch of suspects to be called.

DO NOT FORGET THEM

Note down the time and date when you called them on your call sheet and add them to your list of people to be called later in the next batch. Having already contacted them once (although with no actual conversation) it will break the "cold-call" barrier that exists when people have to call somebody they have never spoken to before. Recycle this contact and don't forget to come back to it.

If, when you do eventually speak to the contact, the answer you receive is a "No" then you have your scripts for reference to see if you can rebuff the rejection and try to turn them around. If not, then as I have said earlier, a customer that says "No" is actually really meaning to say "No, not now, but later". Add this suspect to your list for re-calling in 6 months from now – put it into a later phase of your prospecting work.

If your call results in a false-positive response - the "send me more information" response, then you need to learn to turn this into a strong positive outcome.

All too often the caller takes the path of least resistance and agrees to send information to the prospect and then lamely indicates that they will call the prospect back, once they have had a chance to digest the information, in a week or so perhaps

This is delaying the inevitable rejection – the prospect will almost never be available to meet up or take the follow-up call and if they do happen to read your information, it will be quickly forgotten as they get so much information sent to them by your competitors.

But in my experience there is only ONE WAY to deal with this request. I recommend that you politely tell the caller that you would prefer to drop them information in person and suggest a quick 10 minute time, or suggest a quick informal coffee, to run them through the highlights as you know they are busy.

This approach guarantees to set you apart from your competitors and will ensure that you get some "face to face time" with the prospect, albeit it a small amount of their time. You will then be in a stronger position to articulate your company's value proposition. It places you ahead of your competitors and shows dedication, professionalism and commitment.

They are never there and never call me back

This is a common problem that sales people have and relatively simple to address in 2 distinct ways – the first one means that you recycle that contact and add them to the list to be called at a later date with a different (and hopefully more compelling) offer, the other way is to get another colleague in the office to call for you – an approach that I use as a last resort, only if I believe I truly have an offer that is too compelling for the customer to reasonably ignore.

Basically, your colleague calls up the prospect on the basis that they are seeking information to help them either develop an offer, research some market information or benchmark your performance. Asking a prospect for help, enables them to perhaps disclose why they are unhappy, have not called you back, or what their current problem is.

TO DO

- [ ] Before calling refer to the sheet *"Rewarding My Achievements"* and focus on the outcome of all your hard work
- [ ] Start calling through Batch 1 and maintain focus as you call through subsequent batches
- [ ] Remember to time the length of each call
- [ ] Remember to talk slower, whilst lowering the tone and pitch of your voice
- [ ] Keep an accurate record of the conversation and note data from each call for future reference.
- [ ] Record call progress and info in CRM system (if appropriate)
- [ ] Personalise the scripts for your own use, on the basis of feedback from successful and unsuccessful calls
- [ ] Constantly refine scripts to become even more effective
- [ ] Plan, Plan, Plan
- [ ] Practice, Practice, Practice
- [ ] Keep motivated and focus on hitting your sales target

CHAPTER 7

Leaving voicemail

If you are making the calls and following the methodology set out in this book, then chances are that you are going to have to leave messages or voicemail for some of the people you have to call – let's face it, they won't all be in first time to take your calls and there will be times when their phones will divert to voicemail.

I believe that you should always leave a message or voicemail – there is a possibility (however small) that the contact may actually call you back– after all, sales is a numbers game! However, the best reason for leaving a message or voicemail is that if you leave the right message then you greatly increase the chances of getting that meeting, and by implication you increase the chance of a sale.

The object of any message or voicemail must be to make the listener interested to call you back, make them interested to take your call next time and ultimately agree to buy from you.

There are two basic methodologies that I use and they both work effectively – one relies on the art of referral and the other is a methodology that always guarantees success and plays on the human instinct of curiosity.

REFERRAL VOICEMAIL

Leaving a referral voicemail is becoming increasingly commonplace and essentially uses the success you have had with another company, to gain the listeners trust and get them to call you back.

So, when leaving a message or voicemail you need to refer to the company with whom you have had success – but crucially, you do not mention any more than the name of that company – they will be intrigued and will be compelled to call back.

Make sure you:

1. Speak slowly in a softer tone, and do not speed up as you are worried the voicemail will cut out.
2. Know what you are going to say when you leave that message.
3. Remember to leave your name, your phone number, your company's name and the referral company you are calling about.

When they do call back, you will be in a position to use one of the scripts you have prepared earlier and taken the caller through your pitch – but remember to ask for that meeting.

I have trained people to use this type of script several times and, at this stage, there are several areas of caution that you need to be aware of – THESE ARE CRUCIAL.

Do not be economic with the truth, but make certain you are clear that you are calling from your company but your call concerns Company A. If you don't do that, then you will get into trouble later and sabotage the sale completely – be truthful, but careful.

When picking the company to refer to, it doesn't really matter if they are large or small – in fact, it doesn't really matter if anybody particularly knows that company. The key thing is, to encourage the suspect to call back.

Chances are, the suspect will say, "I don't even know them", and you can start to say, "Well, they do XYZ. Anyway, the reason I was contacting you was……" and off you go on your script…

'USE THEIR CURIOSITY' VOICEMAIL

This method is something that I have developed over several years and it is a method that has been used in the recruitment industry for decades.

Deep down, we all want to feel recognised and respected, and unless you are totally satisfied in your job, you will entertain a call from what appears to be a "head-hunter" – somebody who mysteriously calls you or leaves you a message and asked you to call "John Smith" – yet leaves not further information than that.

This approach is similar, and plays on that sentiment, it does not offer a job, but a means of encouraging the prospect to call you back.

script

Referral Voicemail

Use this script if you have to leave a message and want them to call you back

Leaving message with a secretary, PA or support staff:

This is _____ from _____.
      (Insert your name)   (Insert company name)

My telephone number is _____.
      (Insert your phone number)

Would you please tell _____ that it's regarding
      (Insert name of contact)

_____.
(Insert name of company in the same sector that you have had success with)

Leaving Voicemail:

This is _____ from _____.
      (Insert your name)   (Insert company name)

My telephone number is _____.
      (Insert your phone number)

I am phoning regarding _____.
      (Insert name of company in the same sector that you have had success with)

script

Curiosity Voicemail

Use this script if you have to leave a message and want them to call you back

Leaving message with a secretary, PA or support staff:

This is _____ from _____.
           (Insert your name)   (Insert your company name)

My telephone number is _____.
                          (Insert your phone number)

Would you please ask _____ to call me?
                     (Insert name of your contact)

Leaving a voicemail:

This is _____ from _____.
           (Insert your name)   (Insert your company name)

My telephone number is _____.
                          (Insert your name)

I was wondering if you could give me a call back when you have 5 minutes for a private chat.

TO DO

- ☐ Breathe deeply and speak slowly as you make the call
- ☐ Remember to stand up and smile when you call
- ☐ Make sure you have referred to the specifically tailored value proposition for the functional manager you are calling
- ☐ Plan what you will say when leaving messages, with particular reference to my scripts
- ☐ Be specific whilst not giving too much away
- ☐ Note down, on the calling sheet or CRM tool, when you left a message, what you said and what you wanted to say

CHAPTER 8

Gordon Gekko

Have you seen the film, "Wall Street", directed by Oliver Stone, starring Michael Douglas and Charlie Sheen ?

Avoiding the obvious focus on clichés about money and greed, the film provides a good lesson for anybody trying to set appointments, avoid a gatekeeper and breakthrough.

In the film, the main character, Bud Fox, repeatedly tries to set an appointment with the film's main character – Gordon Gekko – obviously trying to sell him something. He calls daily, is knocked-back by the harsh "gatekeeper" (but if he had read this book he may have done a little better and perhaps have called during the Golden Hour), and is eventually rewarded with a meeting, which leads to great riches and success and eventual downfall.

However....what can we learn from what Bud did?

1. Bud was persistent – knowing Gordon Gecko's birthday having conducted extensive research on the person he was trying to meet with, knowing the name of his PA etc. He obviously maintained a great CRM system.
2. He called regularly and politely – we see him calling early in the day and being persistent.
3. He had done his pre-research about who he was calling – the individual, his company, their news, the market dynamics, the detail of the people he was going to meet. He was thoroughly prepared.
4. But…when he got that meeting, he had failed to prepare – but he did get that meeting. He had no clear value proposition when pressured to articulate his value to Gordon Gekko and stumbled. He eventually relied on a weak value proposition (founded on insider knowledge) which ended in disaster.

Applying much of what Bud Fox does, really emulates much of what you have learned in this book. Namely:

- Research – Know who you are calling, information about them, company information and industry trends.
- Relevance – Understand what value you can add to their business and what value you will add.
- Persistence – Don't be put off if they say no. Just recycle them for another time.
- Prepare – Prepare your elevator pitch with friends and colleagues and make sure it is crisp, meaningful and focussed.

CHAPTER 9

A life less ordinary

If you are reading this last chapter and put into practice everything I have told you so far, then the chances are that you are starting to see a real improvement in your sales results and dreaming of a life less ordinary.

Understanding that sales is inherently all about the numbers and ratios that requires dedication and focus, will almost certainly make you a sales superstar – but the key thing is to maintain that focus and momentum. There is absolutely no benefit in starting on this course of action and then stopping – keep calling, monitor your progress and constantly strive to be the best sales person there is. Persistent focus on improving guarantees you will be successful.

Once you have started, make certain that you are not stale – constantly update your scripts, change your approach, call new customers in a new way, but most of all, make sure that you continue to visualise that success. Go back and benchmark your performance using the *Funnel of Truth*. I find it helpful to see how I am tracking in relation to my past performance – Am I improving? Is my call to meetings ratio improving? Am I making more money? Am I more successful? Am I meeting more decision makers more often?

Key elements that you need to remember:

1. Call during the Golden Hour – 08:00 – 09:00 or the Silver Hour – 17:45 – 18:45.
2. Plan your calls – Use my scripts as the basis for making calls, and refine them for your particular circumstances.
3. Know your "Recipe" – Ensure you are targeting the correct customer base – speak to your marketing division and your colleagues; replicate the same types of companies and contacts the successful people in your business are focussing on.
4. Prepare before you call – You need to do your background homework on the company; utilise the internet, networking sites, trade bodies and the press to research. When you make the call this way you will quickly demonstrate knowledge, expertise and good "pitch" angle for your solution.
5. Ask for the meeting- If you don't ask, you won't get.
6. Remember why you are calling – You are calling to meet your sales targets, become a sales superstar and reward yourself with something you have always wanted.
7. Remain positive – It is not always easy to keep calling; some prospects will be rude and say "No". Remain positive, no just means "Not now". Diarise as another opportunity to follow up at a later date.

If you follow the basic principles contained in this book and continually review what works for you, you will start to see an improvement in your figures; this will keep you positive and focussed and enable you to buy your fast car, luxury cruise or palatial home sooner than you think. And above all remember:

••

SUCCESS BREEDS SUCCESS

••

ABOUT THE AUTHOR

Nicholas McMenemy is an expert in the fields of sales and business development and has extensive expertise in working with high-performing sales teams across Europe, North America, and Asia, specifically focused in the telecoms and technology markets. Nicholas has previously held management positions with organizations including British Telecom, Concert and Westcon Group, as well as several successful start-up organizations.

www.ingramcontent.com/pod-product-compliance
Lightning Source LLC
Chambersburg PA
CBHW051813170526
45167CB00005B/2001